# You Are Not Broken: A Practical Guide to Healing Avoidant Attachment

Michelle Carbone, CCHt

Copyright © 2025 Michelle Carbone

All rights reserved.

ISBN: 979-8-9939058-0-8

# CONTENTS

**Notes**

**Introduction: You Are Not Broken – Page 5**

**Chapter 1 – Page 9**
Understanding Disorganized (Fearful-Avoidant) & Dismissive (Avoidant) Attachment

**Chapter 2 – Page 17**
The Subconscious Mind and the Roots of Avoidance

**Chapter 3 – Page 27**
The Nervous System: Healing Begins in the Body

**Chapter 4 – Page 37**
Transforming Thought Patterns—Changing the Avoidant Mind

**Integration Moment – Page 45**
Honoring How Far You've Come

**Chapter 5 – Page 47**
From Noticing to Nurturing—Mindfulness and Somatic Practices

**Chapter 6 – Page 55**
Reparenting Your Inner Child—Building the Safety You Never Had

**Chapter 7 – Page 63**
Cultivating Emotional Safety in Relationships

**Chapter 8 – Page 69**
When Triggers Happen—Growing Through Setbacks

**Chapter 9 – Page 77**
Becoming Secure—Recognizing Progress and Anchoring Healing

**Final Chapter / Bonus Section – Page 83**
Daily Practices for Lasting Healing & Connection

**Thank You – Page 87**

**About the Author – Page - 89**

## A Note on Blame and the People We Hurt (and Who Hurt Us)

As you read this book, you may notice stories or reflections about my childhood, my family, or others who shaped my journey. I want you to know: this is not about blame or making anyone "wrong." I believe, as taught in A Course in Miracles and many spiritual traditions, that we each come into this life with soul agreements—opportunities to learn, heal, and grow, sometimes through challenge and contrast.

The people in my story, and in yours, were doing the best they could with the awareness and resources they had. My intention is not to judge or hold resentment, but to understand, forgive, and transform. Healing is not about assigning fault. It's about reclaiming your power, your wholeness, and your ability to love—yourself, and even those who could not love you in the ways you needed.

This journey of healing is also about forgiving yourself: for the times you may have hurt others, knowingly or unknowingly, while acting from your own pain, confusion, or fear. We are all learning together. May this journey be one of compassion, not only for yourself, but for everyone who played a role in your becoming.

## A Note on Terminology

You may notice that attachment styles can be called by different names in various books or resources. For clarity and consistency throughout this guide, I'll be using the terms **Dismissive (Avoidant)** and **Disorganized (Fearful-Avoidant)** to describe the two main avoidant attachment patterns I focus on.
Other sources may refer to Dismissive as "Avoidant," or Disorganized as "Fearful-Avoidant" or even "Anxious-Avoidant." While the labels may differ, the core experiences and healing practices remain the same.
No matter what words are used, remember: your patterns are not a life sentence—they are simply starting points on your journey of understanding, compassion, and change

# INTRODUCTION: YOU ARE NOT BROKEN

*My past shaped me, but it does not define me.*

When I was a child, I sat in my room, quietly hoping someone would notice. Hoping someone would ask me the right questions — the ones that would unlock the feelings I didn't know how to express or process.
I longed for connection, especially with my father.
I longed for someone to *see me*, to help me open up, to prove that I was worthy of being cared for.
But the questions never came.
And eventually, I learned what so many others have learned: **it's safer not to need anyone.**

This was the beginning of my journey into avoidant attachment — a survival strategy stitched together from longing, fear, and the deep, deep desire to belong.

Maybe you recognize yourself here, too.
Maybe you learned to pull away when you needed someone most.
Maybe you taught yourself that being "independent" meant being untouchable.
Maybe you still find yourself swinging between the hunger for connection and the terror of vulnerability — caught in the confusing dance of Avoidant Attachment - both Disorganized (fearful-avoidant) and Dismissive (avoidant) attachment patterns.

If so, hear me when I say this: **you are not broken.**
Your patterns, no matter how painful they feel now, were once brilliant strategies your mind and body used to protect you.
You survived because of them.
You adapted brilliantly to a world that didn't always meet your needs in the ways you deserved.

But now, survival is no longer enough.
You are ready to live.
You are ready to love — yourself first, and then others, in ways that feel safe, nourishing, and true.

This book is a roadmap home.
It is a journey through the mind, the body, the nervous system, the subconscious — all the places where your deepest patterns were formed and all the places where they can be healed.

**You'll learn:**

- How Disorganized (fearful-avoidant) and Dismissive (avoidant) attachments are formed — and how they quietly shape your thoughts, reactions, and relationships.

- How to gently rewire your subconscious mind, making safety and connection *familiar* again.

- How your nervous system, particularly your vagus nerve, holds the keys to feeling safe in love, life, and intimacy.

- How somatic work, mindfulness, and intuitive connection with your body can heal wounds that thinking alone cannot reach.

- How to re-parent the younger you who never got the safety and love they needed — and how to meet those needs now, with tenderness and strength.

**Along the way, I'll share stories from my own journey and those of my clients:**

- How early hypnotherapy sessions began to gently unwind old patterns of self-protection and open my heart to healing.

- How learning to tune into my body transformed the way I experience love, trust, and emotional safety—moment by moment.

- How real, embodied safety is discovered not just in thoughts, but through the breath, heartbeat, and subtle cues of the nervous system.

- How small, consistent shifts—whether a mindful pause, a new boundary, or a compassionate word to yourself—can gradually rewire your mind, body, and relationships.

- And how setbacks, triggers, and moments of self-doubt are not failures, but invitations to practice new tools and build self-trust, one step at a time.

**You are not too broken. You are not too late.
You are not too much or too little.**

*You are a divine being, worthy of love —
and most importantly, worthy of feeling safe to love.*

Let's begin the journey home to yourself.

# CHAPTER 1:

# UNDERSTANDING DISORGANIZED (FEARFUL-AVOIDANT) AND DISMISSIVE (AVOIDANT) ATTACHMENT STYLES

**What Is Attachment?**

Before we talk about avoidant attachment styles, let's get clear on what *attachment* actually means.

**Attachment** is the deep, instinctive bond that forms between a child and their primary caregivers. It's how we learn—often unconsciously—what to expect from others, and what others will expect from us.

Our earliest attachment experiences shape how we relate to ourselves, to other people, and even to life itself.

There are several core attachment styles:

- **Secure attachment:** Feeling safe to reach out, trust, and receive love.

- **Anxious attachment:** Fearing abandonment and needing constant reassurance.

- **Dismissive (Avoidant) attachment:** Downplaying needs, prioritizing independence, and often disconnecting emotionally.

- **Disorganized (fearful-avoidant) attachment:** Craving closeness but fearing it, leading to a confusing push-pull dynamic.

Most people are a blend, but we each have a *dominant style*—and it can shift over time or with different people.

**Why Attachment Styles Matter**

Attachment is at the root of everything from how we handle conflict, to how we show affection, to how we set (or struggle with) boundaries. If you've ever wondered why you keep repeating the same relationship patterns, or why intimacy can feel so scary or draining, attachment is a huge piece of that puzzle.
When our early environment was emotionally unpredictable, critical, unsafe, or unavailable, we often develop protective adaptations—what we now call attachment *styles*. These adaptations aren't "bad"—they are creative solutions your younger self came up with to survive and get by.

**Disorganized (Fearful-Avoidant) Attachment—
The Push-Pull Experience**

Disorganized attachment, also called **fearful-avoidant**, is the most confusing and distressing of the attachment styles.

**Common Traits:**

- Deep desire for connection, closeness, and love

- Simultaneous fear of being hurt, rejected, criticized, or abandoned

- Difficulty trusting others and self

- Intense emotional ups and downs in relationships

- Tendency to "test" people, withdraw, or become anxious, then pull close again

**What It Feels Like:**

Living with disorganized attachment is like having one foot on the gas and one on the brake at all times.
You want love desperately, but when it arrives, you feel threatened, unworthy, or suffocated.
You may find yourself sabotaging relationships, picking fights, or suddenly pulling away for no clear reason—even when things are going well.

**Where It Comes From:**

Disorganized attachment often arises when a child's caregiver is both a source of comfort and a source of fear or unpredictability. Maybe there was abuse, but sometimes it's simply emotional inconsistency, a parent who was loving but overwhelmed, or family chaos that left you unsure what to expect.
The child learns: *"I need you, but I can't trust you. I want closeness, but closeness is dangerous."*

**Dismissive (Avoidant) Attachment—The Lone Wolf Strategy**

Dismissive avoidant attachment is sometimes described as the "lone wolf" style.

**Common Traits:**

- Strong sense of independence, often to the point of isolation

- Downplaying or denying emotional needs ("I'm fine on my own")

- Difficulty expressing feelings, especially vulnerable ones

- Feeling uncomfortable when others get too close or "clingy"

- Prioritizing logic and self-sufficiency over emotional connection

**What It Feels Like:**

For the dismissive avoidant, intimacy can feel threatening—not because they don't want love, but because it feels safer to depend on themselves.
Often, there's a sense of pride in being "unaffected," but underneath, there's usually loneliness, old grief, and a fear of being let down.

**Where It Comes From:**

Dismissive avoidant attachment often grows from a childhood where needs were minimized, dismissed, or met with discomfort. Maybe you were praised for being "the easy child," for not needing too much, for handling things yourself.
Or maybe showing emotion was met with coldness, ridicule, or withdrawal from caregivers.
The child learns: *"Needing is unsafe. The less I need, the safer I am. I don't have to depend on anyone."*

**Both Styles—A Common Core of Loneliness**

Disorganized and dismissive avoidant styles can *look* different on the surface, but both are rooted in **self-protection and fear of being hurt**.

- Both may fear abandonment or engulfment.

- Both struggle to trust themselves and others fully.

- Both often feel unseen, misunderstood, or fundamentally alone.

And both styles are **adaptations, not defects**.
They are creative, protective responses to environments where being emotionally open just wasn't safe or supported.

## How These Patterns Show Up in Adult Life

- **In romantic relationships:** Sabotaging closeness, "ghosting," jumping into or out of relationships quickly, withdrawing after conflict or intimacy, feeling suffocated by too much attention.

- **With friends:** Struggling to maintain closeness, rarely asking for help, keeping secrets, disappearing when things get too intense.

- **At work or in groups:** Avoiding teamwork, feeling like an outsider, fearing feedback, or being hyper-independent.

- **With self:** Harsh inner critic, difficulty naming or soothing feelings, chronic loneliness even in a crowd.

## My Own Experience - Longing to Be Seen

As a child, I remember wanting to open up, to be seen, feel important and know I was good enough. I didn't know how to open up or ask for help. I wished someone would ask me the right questions and insist on hearing my truth - or help me find my truth. Instead, silence and emotional distance became normal.

Relationships were surface level. I always appeared to be happy (I was the good girl, after all) and I certainly was happy at times, as we all are. And, there was an underlying sadness that I wasn't able to explain or express and that I easily ignored and pushed away. I was quite disconnected from any difficult feelings most of the time - anger, sadness, grief… These were all emotions I did not know how to feel or process and my mind did me a favor by disconnecting me from feeling them.

In my adult relationships, I longed for connection but found myself unable to express myself when there were issues I wanted to bring up, I'd run away (emotionally or physically) or freeze/shut down when things got real. I would pull away, then panic that I'd be abandoned, then come close again. I'd try to be who they wanted me to be, terrified they would leave me, even when somewhere inside I knew I wasn't happy and really, I wanted them to go. I was a people pleaser and co-dependent. I wanted someone to love me and see me and would do whatever I needed to in order to have someone stay. It took me years to realize what I was even doing and feeling and to understand that these weren't character flaws—they were old survival strategies, still running my life. When I began to understand attachment, everything started to make sense. It was the first step in forgiving myself and beginning real change.

**Why Naming Your Style Matters (But Doesn't Define You)**

Naming your dominant attachment style is powerful—not because you need another "label," but because it helps you:

- Normalize your experience ("Oh, that's why I do this!")
- Find the right healing tools
- Move from shame to compassion

**You are not your attachment style.**

You are a living, growing, healing human being—capable of new patterns and secure love.

**Reflection Questions**

1. Which of these traits or experiences do I recognize in myself?

2. How do I usually react when someone gets emotionally close to me? What about when I feel rejected or unseen?

3. What old messages did I get about needing, feeling, or depending on others?

4. When was the last time I felt safe to show up as myself, without fear of judgment or abandonment?

## Chapter 1 Summary and Next Steps

If you see yourself in these patterns, you are not alone—and you are not broken.

You learned to adapt for good reason. The journey ahead is about *unlearning what no longer serves you* and building a foundation of true safety, within and with others.

In the next chapter, we'll explore how these patterns get "wired in" at the subconscious level—and how you can begin gently, powerfully rewiring them for a new experience of love.

### Affirmation:

**I am allowed to understand my patterns with compassion.
I am not defined by my past.
Every moment is a new chance to love and be loved.**

# CHAPTER 2:

# THE SUBCONSCIOUS MIND AND THE ROOTS OF AVOIDANCE

### Why We Do What We Do (Even When We Don't Want To)

Have you ever found yourself reacting in ways you know don't serve you—but you just can't seem to stop?
Maybe you ghost someone you actually like.
Maybe you feel intense anxiety the moment a relationship deepens.
Maybe you stay distant even though you're longing to be seen.
It can feel confusing, even frustrating.
*Why do I keep doing this?* you might ask yourself.
*Why can't I just be normal?*

The answer lies not in conscious willpower or logic.
It lives in the realm of the **subconscious mind**—the place where your attachment patterns were first formed.

### What Is the Subconscious Mind?
### (And Why Does It Run the Show?)

Your subconscious mind is like a vast, powerful operating system running quietly in the background of your life. It stores everything you've ever learned, witnessed, or experienced—especially in early childhood, when your brain was in a highly absorbent, hypnotic state.

At its core, the subconscious mind has one mission:
**Keep you safe.**

But here's the catch: The subconscious doesn't measure "safety" the way your adult self would. It measures safety based on what is *familiar*—not necessarily what is *healthy* or *good* for you. **Safe simply means it didn't kill you.**

**The mind loves what is familiar and avoids what is unfamiliar.**
*~Marisa Peer*

Learning this "Rule of the Mind" by Marisa Peer changed my life—and it can change yours too.

### Neuroscience:
### How the Brain Builds (and Maintains) Patterns

When you were little, your brain was wiring itself at lightning speed. **Neuroplasticity**—your brain's ability to form new pathways—means every repeated emotional experience, every way you responded to stress, and every method you used to get (or avoid) love became deeply rooted.

### Key players in your brain:

- **Amygdala:** Your emotional alarm bell. If relationships felt threatening, it learned to sound the alarm with even small reminders.

- **Hippocampus:** Stores your memories, including what "danger" feels like. It helps your brain quickly spot and react to similar situations, even if they're no longer unsafe.

- **Prefrontal Cortex:** The rational, calming "parent" of your brain. In childhood, this part isn't fully developed, so big feelings and alarms from the amygdala run the show.

- **Vagus Nerve:** Links your brain and body, sending signals when you're safe or under threat (more on this in the next chapter).

Every time you pulled away, numbed out, or hid your needs, you laid down a "survival pathway." Your brain rewarded you with relief (however short-lived), reinforcing the cycle. Over time, these responses became almost automatic—*habits of the brain and body.*

**Modern neuroscience shows:**

- You're not broken or weak—your brain is doing exactly what it learned to do.

- The more you repeat a pattern, the stronger and faster the neural "trail" becomes (like wearing a groove in a record).

- The GOOD NEWS: *Neuroplasticity* means you can gently create new, healthier trails—at any age.

**How Attachment Patterns Get Installed**

When you were little, you were like a sponge.
You absorbed the emotional climate around you, even when you didn't have words for what you felt.

You learned:

- Is it safe to cry?

- Is it safe to ask for help?

- Is it safe to be excited, loud, or full of life?

- Is it safe to be imperfect?

Depending on the answers your environment gave you, your subconscious mind developed strategies to keep you safe:

- **If love felt inconsistent or frightening**, you may have become Disorganized (Fearful-Avoidant).

- **If emotional needs were dismissed or ignored**, you may have become Dismissive (Avoidant).

These strategies were brilliant at the time. But now, as an adult, they can become barriers to the deep connection and peace you long for.

**The Good News:
You Can Rewire Your Subconscious (and Your Brain!)**

Here's the beautiful truth:

**What your mind once learned, it can unlearn.
What your body once feared, it can befriend.
What your heart once armored, it can open again.**

Your brain remains neuroplastic throughout life!

This means:

- Every time you try a new response—even something tiny—you're laying the foundation for a new, healthier "trail."

- Mindfulness, self-awareness, and compassion *downshift* the brain's threat response and make new learning possible.

- *Repetition* is key—small steps, repeated with care, are more powerful than "big leaps" you can't sustain.

**Personal Story: How I Started Unwinding My Old Patterns**

When I first started training as a Rapid Transformational Therapist, I began noticing how deeply my mind clung to old, familiar patterns of protection.

I would automatically shut down when conversations got emotional or when I wanted to express myself, but would be overcome by fear. I would pull away from people who showed they cared about me. But during my first few hypnotherapy sessions—both as a client and as a trainee—I noticed subtle but powerful shifts.

I realized I could *choose* to see things differently. I could *choose* to feel differently. One session in particular opened my eyes:

I saw clearly that my mind wasn't my enemy—it was trying to protect me, based on outdated instructions.
Learning that gave me a gift of allowing compassion for myself.
I wasn't broken. I was beautifully, brilliantly adapted.
And if I could adapt once, I could adapt again—this time toward love, safety, and belonging.

## A Client Story: The Smallest Step

"Amy," a client, spent years running from closeness. Her body panicked at signs of real connection.
In our work together, she practiced one tiny experiment: stay present for a few extra seconds during a difficult conversation.
She wrote me later: "My heart was pounding, but I stayed. I didn't run. Afterward, I was shaky, but also kind of proud."
That small moment laid the first new trail in her brain. Over time, those little wins built confidence—and more moments of real connection.

## Reprogramming the Subconscious: The Basics

Here are a few key ways we'll work with your subconscious mind throughout this book:

- **Awareness:** Recognizing old patterns without judgment. Be curious!

- **Affirmations:** Repeating new truths until they become familiar.

- **Somatic Practices:** Using body awareness to shift emotional states and send safety signals to the brain.

•

- **Hypnotic Visualization:** Speaking directly to the subconscious in its own language (images, feelings, repetition).

- **Mindfulness:** Catching reactive thoughts and choosing new ones.

- **Inner Child Healing:** Reparenting the parts of you that learned fear or withdrawal.

Healing is not about erasing your past. It's about creating new possibilities for your future—gently, one choice at a time.

# Neuroscience-Informed Exercises

## Spot the Survival Pathway

**Purpose:** Build awareness of your automatic responses—without judgment.

- Next time you feel triggered or start to withdraw, PAUSE.

- Notice: Is this my "old pathway" firing up? (Maybe your heart races, you get irritable, you freeze, or want to run.)

- Say silently or out loud:

    "Hello, old protector. Thank you for keeping me safe all these years. I'm learning a new way."

## The 90-Second Reset

Based on brain science, an intense emotion usually rises and falls in about 90 seconds if you allow it (Jill Bolte Taylor, neuroscientist).

- When you're overwhelmed, set a timer for 90 seconds.

- Breathe slowly, put a hand on your heart or belly.

- Notice where the feeling is in your body. Don't analyze, just feel.

- When the timer is up, gently ask:
  "What do I need right now? Can I try a new response?"

**Rewire with Repetition**

- Pick ONE new thought, behavior, or self-soothing gesture (e.g., "I am safe with gentle closeness" + place hand on heart).

- Repeat it every day for 2 weeks, especially when you catch the old pattern.

- Track: What feels different? When does the new "trail" feel a tiny bit easier?


**Micro-Exposure to Connection**

- Identify one person or setting where you feel safest (or at least not threatened).

- Practice a small, safe act of connection: make eye contact, share a small truth, stay present for one more breath.

- Celebrate even the smallest success.

- Note: This is real, physical brain rewiring at work!

**Practice: Making the Unfamiliar Familiar**

Each day, notice a moment when you want to default to an old pattern—like pulling away, numbing out, or dismissing your needs.

- Pause.

- Ask yourself:

    o What's the familiar story here?

    o What new, loving action can I choose instead—even if it feels strange?

- Pair your new choice with a calming action (breath, touch, posture).

Repeat:
**"I am choosing to [feel/express/try/trust], and I am choosing to feel great about it."**


**Reflection Exercise: Meeting Your Subconscious**

Take a few moments to breathe deeply.

Close your eyes if it feels safe. Then ask yourself:

- What old beliefs about love, trust, or connection might my subconscious still be holding onto?

- Where might I be choosing familiarity over happiness?

- What new beliefs would I like to teach my mind—starting now?

### Quote to Hold in Your Heart:

*The first step to change is awareness. The second step is acceptance. The third is choosing differently, again and again, with love.*


### Remember:

"*I am choosing to heal, and I am choosing to feel great about it.*"


### Final Words for Chapter 2

You are not broken.
You are beautifully, brilliantly adapted.
Your brain, mind, and body are ready for change—one small, loving moment at a time.


**Next:**
In Chapter 3, we'll explore how your nervous system and vagus nerve shape your sense of safety—and how to gently help your body feel at home with connection.

# CHAPTER 3:

# THE NERVOUS SYSTEM: HEALING BEGINS IN THE BODY

**Your Body Remembers**

Healing your attachment style isn't just a mental or emotional process—it's a deeply physical one too. Even when you logically understand your patterns, your body might still react automatically with tension, anxiety, or numbness.
This is because trauma, abandonment wounds, and emotional neglect aren't just stored in your mind—they live in your nervous system.
Your nervous system is the bridge between what you feel and how you act. And when it's been wired for survival, it can misinterpret even safe, loving situations as threats. If we want real, lasting change, we have to include the body in the conversation.

**Understanding Your Nervous System**

At its core, your nervous system has two major modes:

- **Fight/Flight:** Activated when there's perceived danger—you feel anxious, restless, defensive, angry, urgent.

- **Freeze/Fawn:** Activated when danger feels overwhelming—you might feel numb, disconnected, paralyzed, overly accommodating to others.

When you have a Disorganized (Fearful-Avoidant) or Dismissive (Avoidant) attachment style, you often switch between these modes without fully realizing it.

You might "numb out" emotionally during conflict (freeze), overwork yourself to feel needed (fawn), or get agitated and anxious when someone gets too close (flight).

Your body is trying to protect you—even when no real threat exists.
**The Science: Why Your Body Reacts Before Your Mind**

Let's go deeper.

Your nervous system is always scanning for cues of safety and danger—a process neuroscientist Stephen Porges calls **neuroception**. If, as a child, you experienced emotional chaos, neglect, or criticism, your body learned to brace for threat, even if that threat was "only" emotional.

Your **amygdala** (the brain's alarm bell) gets trained to respond to any cue of closeness or emotion as potential danger. Your **vagus nerve** helps regulate how quickly you can return to calm—but if your system spent years in fight/flight or freeze, it may overreact or struggle to recover.

The **polyvagal theory** teaches us there's more than just "fight or flight"—there's also "freeze" and "fawn." These show up as dissociation, numbness, people-pleasing, or collapsing, especially when overwhelm feels inescapable.

**The Role of the Vagus Nerve**

One of the most important players in your body's experience of safety is the **vagus nerve**—the longest cranial nerve in your body, running from your brainstem down through your face, heart, lungs, and gut.

The vagus nerve helps regulate your:

- Breathing
- Heartbeat
- Digestion
- Emotional state
- Social engagement (how "safe" you feel with others)

When your vagus nerve is healthy and activated (what's called "ventral vagal tone"), you feel:

- Calm
- Open
- Connected
- Capable of handling challenges

When it's underactive or overstrained, you might feel:

- Chronically anxious
- Disconnected from yourself and others
- Hypervigilant or shut down
- Emotionally reactive

**The beautiful news?**

You can train your nervous system to feel safer—just like you can reprogram your mind.

## Trusting My Body's Wisdom

I didn't realize for a long time that my body had been talking to me all along. For years, my mind was racing, but I was completely disconnected from what I was feeling physically. It wasn't until I went through an intensive intuitive coaching program that I began focusing on practicing mindfulness and somatic awareness.

Slowly, I learned to tune in:
I could notice when my body felt safe and open—or when it tensed and withdrew.

Later, when I met a new partner who created real emotional safety, I noticed something powerful: My body would feel relaxed, soft, and peaceful around him. But when small ruptures happened, or something triggered an old fear, my body would tell me immediately through anxiety, tension, or tears.

Learning to trust these signals changed my entire relationship with myself. It gave me a way to recognize safety (or the lack of it) before my mind even caught up. It was like reconnecting with an inner compass I never knew I had.

## Client Story: "Shaking Off the Past"

"Daniel" always described himself as "chill." He'd learned to keep everything bottled up, never letting himself get too close or too angry. But inside, he was often anxious, tense, and would find himself dissociating—losing time or feeling numb when things got intense.

In our work together, Daniel began to notice what happened in his body when a partner got emotional or asked for deeper connection. His chest would tighten, his shoulders tense, his legs feel heavy.

Instead of trying to talk himself out of these feelings, he started experimenting with gentle somatic practices—breathing, stretching, shaking out his hands, even just humming.

Over time, he realized his "chill" was actually a freeze response. As he learned to let his body feel and release energy safely, he discovered new emotions under the surface—grief, fear, and eventually, relief. He began to trust himself to stay present, even during difficult conversations. His body learned: it was safe to feel, safe to be here, safe to connect.

## How Somatic Work Heals (A Deeper Dive)

- **Your nervous system is always scanning for cues of safety and danger—even before your mind is aware.**

- Safe touch, mindful breathing, and gentle movement send calming signals to the amygdala and vagus nerve, telling your brain, *"It's okay now."*

- Repeated safe somatic experiences build new neural pathways. With time, your body can learn to respond with openness and calm, not just survival.

## Key science points:

- The more often you experience *real* safety (even in small doses), the stronger the neural pathways for calm and connection become.

- Safe eye contact, soft voice, and gentle touch activate your social nervous system, helping you "co-regulate" with safe people.

- Mindful body awareness activates your insular cortex—helping you spot your survival modes sooner, so you can gently shift.

## Simple Practices to Regulate Your Nervous System

You don't need elaborate routines to start healing. Small daily practices can make a huge difference:

### Deep Belly Breathing

- 3–5 slow breaths into your belly can shift you out of fight/flight.

### Vagus Nerve Toning

- Humming, singing, gargling, or chanting stimulate the vagus nerve.

### Cold Water Splash

- Splashing cold water on your face or taking a brisk shower activates the vagus nerve and resets your system.

### Grounding Techniques

- Press your feet firmly into the ground, hold a comforting object, or focus on physical sensations to anchor yourself in the present.

### Mindful Touch

- Gently place your hand over your heart or belly to signal safety and self-compassion.

### Co-Regulation

- Spending time with safe, calm people can regulate your nervous system through connection.

## More Somatic Safety Practices

### "Orienting" (Body + Brain Reset)

- Look around and name 5 things you see, 4 you can touch, 3 you hear, 2 you smell, 1 you taste/remember tasting. This signals safety to your brain.

### "Shake It Out"

- Animals literally "shake off" stress—humans can, too! Shake your hands, arms, legs, or whole body to discharge tension.

### "Body Scan for Safety"

- Slowly scan your body from head to toe. Where is there tension, heaviness, or numbness? With each breath, imagine sending warmth or a gentle light to those places.

### Advanced Practice: Safe Social Engagement Experiment

**Purpose:** Gently teach your nervous system that small connections can be safe.

1. Choose a very low-stakes social interaction (smiling at a cashier, texting a supportive friend, greeting a neighbor).

2. Before the interaction, place your hand on your heart. Breathe deeply and say: "I am safe to connect for just a moment."

3. During the interaction, notice your breath, make eye contact if possible, and see if you can stay present just a few seconds longer than usual.

4. After, breathe again and notice: Is there relief, tension, numbness, or maybe a spark of connection? Celebrate even the tiniest success.

## Healing Isn't About Never Getting Triggered

It's about recovering faster. It's about noticing, "Ah, my system is activated," and gently offering yourself the safety you need in that moment.
You're not broken if you feel anxious or numb sometimes.
You're human—learning new ways to be.

### Reflection Exercise: Listening to Your Body

Today, take 5–10 minutes to sit quietly and check in with yourself. You might place one hand over your heart, another over your belly.

Ask yourself:

- What sensations do I notice in my body right now?

- Where do I feel tension? Where do I feel ease?

- Is there a part of me that feels unsafe, unworthy, or unloved?

- What would it feel like to offer that part of me safety?

### Quote to Anchor You

"My body is wise. My body is speaking. I am listening with love."

### Gentle Encouragement

Be patient and gentle as you reconnect with your body.
You may encounter numbness, resistance, or strong feelings.
All of this is normal.
You're building a new relationship—with yourself, and with safety.

### Coming Next: Chapter 4 —
How to spot and transform thought
Patterns that keep you stuck in avoidance.

# CHAPTER 4:

# TRANSFORMING THOUGHT PATTERNS—CHANGING THE AVOIDANT MIND

### Your Mind's Old Stories

Healing avoidant attachment doesn't just happen by "thinking positively"—but your thoughts and beliefs do shape your reality. When you've been wired for avoidance, your mind often runs on autopilot, repeating old stories like:

- "It's not safe to need anyone."

- "I'll be rejected if I'm vulnerable."

- "If I get close, I'll lose myself (or get hurt)."

- "No one really wants to know the real me."

These thoughts may have once kept you safe—but now, they keep you stuck in loneliness or anxiety, blocking real intimacy and connection.

### How Thought Patterns Form (and Why They're Hard to Change)

Your thoughts and beliefs are shaped by **neural pathways**—physical patterns in your brain built by repeated experiences and messages from childhood.

If you repeatedly experienced:

- Criticism or withdrawal when showing feelings

- Overwhelm, chaos, or mixed signals from caregivers

- Or learned that love was conditional or unpredictable,

Your mind adapted with protective beliefs to try to keep you safe.

**Neuroscience Fact:**

Every time you repeat a thought ("I can't trust anyone"), the neural pathway gets stronger.
The good news? **Neuroplasticity** means that with intention and repetition, you can form new, healthier thought habits.

**Cognitive Bias and Attachment**

The avoidant mind is wired for self-protection.
Your brain unconsciously scans for evidence to support your core beliefs (this is called *confirmation bias*).
So if you believe "I'm better off alone," your mind will notice and remember times when closeness felt painful, and downplay moments of genuine connection.

**The result?**

Your brain automatically highlights what matches the old story and filters out anything new or contradictory.
But you can gently begin to challenge these biases, and "retrain" your mind to notice new evidence.

**Original Practice: Awareness as the First Step**

Change starts with noticing, not judging. Begin to listen for your mind's stories, especially in moments of stress or intimacy.

Ask yourself:

- "Is this really true? Or is this an old story trying to protect me?"

- "What's another way of looking at this?"

- "What would I tell a beloved friend if they had this thought?"

**Client Story: Rewriting the Script**

"Lisa" (not her real name) came to me after years of avoiding conflict and withdrawing from partners when things got tough. She told herself, "I'm just not good at relationships."
Through our work, Lisa learned to catch the moment when her mind started spinning stories like "This will never work" or "He's going to leave me anyway."
She began a practice of writing down these thoughts, then gently challenging them: "Is that really true? What would happen if I stayed and spoke honestly instead?"
Over time, Lisa built new, more compassionate narratives—like "It's safe to stay, even when it's hard," and "I can express my needs without being abandoned."
These new thoughts didn't erase the old ones overnight, but gradually, Lisa noticed she could stay present, even during tough conversations—and experience a new kind of connection.

**The Science: Changing Your Brain's Story**

Your brain has a powerful "negativity bias"—it's designed to notice threat and repeat old warnings. This was essential for survival, but in modern relationships, it often means your mind fixates on what's wrong, unsafe, or might go badly.

### Brain-based practices to rewire thought patterns:

- **Cognitive Reappraisal:** When you catch a negative thought, pause and ask, "What else could be true here?" This lights up the prefrontal cortex, which helps you reflect and choose differently.

- **Mindful Noting:** Instead of fighting a thought, notice it ("Ah, there's my old 'I'll be abandoned' story"), then let it pass like a cloud. This builds awareness without feeding the old pattern.

- **Positive Evidence Collection:** Write down small moments when you were supported, safe, or accepted—no matter how minor. This retrains your mind to see new evidence for safety and connection.

### Exercise 1: Thought Pattern Journaling

1. For a week, notice when your mind tells you an avoidant or fearful story (e.g., "I can't trust this," "I need to withdraw," "I'm too much for others").

2. Write it down as soon as you notice.

3. Gently ask:
    - "Where did I first learn this?"
    - "Is this true right now, or is it an old fear?"
    - "What's a more compassionate thought I could try?"

4. Practice writing (or saying) the new thought, even if it feels strange.

## Exercise 2: "Thought Reframe Script"

Try this in the moment you notice yourself pulling away or having an avoidant thought:

- Name the thought ("I'm too much.")

- Put your hand on your heart.

- Say: "Thank you, mind, for trying to protect me. I choose to believe I am just right, and it's safe to be myself—even if it feels unfamiliar."

- Breathe deeply and imagine yourself responding from this new place.

## Exercise 3: "If My Mind Were a Friend"

If you notice a harsh or critical thought, pause and imagine that voice as a scared but well-meaning friend.

Ask:
- "What are you trying to protect me from?"

- "What do you need to feel safe letting me try something new?"

Journaling or dialoguing with this "inner protector" helps soften resistance and open up space for new beliefs.

# Reflection Prompts

- What's one thought or belief that shows up most often when I feel triggered or want to withdraw?

- Where did I first learn this story—does it belong to me, or did I inherit it from my family or past?

- What's a small, believable new thought I can practice this week?

- How does my body feel when I try on this new thought?

## Science Spotlight: Self-Compassion and Brain Change

Studies show that practicing self-compassion (noticing pain and responding kindly instead of with criticism) increases activity in the insula and decreases reactivity in the amygdala.

That means:
- When you catch an old thought and respond with kindness ("I'm learning, it's okay"), you literally help your brain feel safer and more open to new beliefs.

## Original Practice: "Mini-Mindfulness Pause"

When you catch yourself spinning in anxious or avoidant thinking:

- Pause and take three slow breaths.

- Notice: "Is my mind predicting the future, replaying the past, or trying to protect me?"

- Say, "In this moment, I am safe. I can choose a new thought, one breath at a time."

## Healing Isn't About Never Having Old Thoughts

Healing is about noticing your patterns, choosing again, and recovering faster each time. You're not broken for having old stories—just human, with a mind that wants to keep you safe.

### Affirmation:

**"Every time I notice an old story, I am creating space for a new one. I am worthy of safe, loving connection."**

### Coming up next: Integration

We'll pause for an "integration moment"—a gentle space to bring together all you've learned so far.
You'll have a chance to reflect, let your insights settle, and anchor the changes you're making in both your mind and body, before moving forward into deeper healing.

# INTEGRATION MOMENT: HONORING HOW FAR YOU'VE COME

Before you continue, take a gentle pause.
You've explored where your patterns began, why your mind protects you, and how your body remembers and responds.
You've started to notice your thoughts, question your beliefs, and imagine new possibilities for connection and safety.

**This is courageous work.**

Even the smallest bit of awareness is a victory—because every new choice begins with noticing.

**Pause and Reflect:**

- What has surprised you most so far about your patterns or your body's wisdom?

- Which new practice or mantra are you most drawn to using in your daily life?

- If you could encourage your younger self right now, what would you say?

**Mini Ritual:**

Place a hand on your heart, take a few slow breaths, and repeat softly:

**I honor every part of me that's shown up for healing.
I am allowed to move at my own pace.
I am safe, I am loved, and I am becoming whole.**

When you're ready, turn the page and step into the next phase of your journey.

**Coming Next: Chapter 5 —**

How to use mindfulness and somatic work to shift from *thinking* to *feeling safe* in your relationships.

# CHAPTER 5:

# FROM NOTICING TO NURTURING—MINDFULNESS AND SOMATIC PRACTICES FOR HEALING AVOIDANT PATTERNS

### Coming Home to the Present

Real healing happens in the here and now. You can't heal the past by only thinking about it—and you can't build a secure future if your mind is always stuck in old stories.

This is where mindfulness and somatic (body-based) practices become your superpowers.

Mindfulness helps you anchor in the present moment, gently noticing what's real right now—rather than reacting to what your mind expects or fears. Somatic practices help you befriend your body, reintroducing a sense of safety, comfort, and connection where there was once tension or numbness.
This chapter is about moving from just noticing your patterns to actually nurturing yourself through them.

**Why Mindfulness Matters for Avoidant Healing**

If you're Disorganized (Fearful-Avoidant) or Dismissive (Avoidant), the present moment can feel elusive or even threatening.
Your mind is trained to scan for danger, replay old hurts, or anticipate disappointment. You can teach your system, gently and gradually, that this moment is safe enough.

**Mindfulness invites you to:**

- Notice your thoughts and feelings without trying to fix or escape them

- Become aware of subtle body sensations and their messages

- Interrupt automatic reactions with a breath, a pause, or a kind word to yourself

- Open up space for new, healing experiences to enter

**The Neuroscience of Mindfulness and Somatic Healing**

When you practice mindfulness, several important shifts happen in your brain and body:

- Your prefrontal cortex (the wise, reflective part of your brain) becomes more active, helping you "pause" before reacting.

- The amygdala (the threat alarm) actually shrinks in volume with regular mindfulness, reducing anxiety and emotional reactivity.

- Practicing present-moment awareness increases the density of gray matter in brain regions involved in self-awareness, emotional regulation, and compassion.

**Somatic practices**—when you connect with your body through breath, touch, or movement—activate your parasympathetic nervous system (rest/digest/safe mode), and calm your vagus nerve, helping your body experience real-time safety.

Research even shows that regular body-based mindfulness can lower baseline cortisol (stress hormone), support immune function, and increase a sense of wellbeing—even for people with a long history of trauma or emotional neglect.

## The Power of Somatic Practices

Somatic work is about experiencing life through your body, not just in your head.
For avoidant styles, this can feel strange or vulnerable at first—especially if you learned to ignore or distrust your body's signals.

**Somatic practices help you:**

- Build trust in your own sensations and intuition

- Calm your nervous system through movement, touch, and breath

- Release old emotions or tension stored in your muscles and cells

- Experience safety and connection as a physical reality, not just an idea

## Client Story: Mindful Moments, Real Change

"Marcus" (not his real name) came to mindfulness with serious skepticism. He told me, "I can't sit still and I don't want to feel my body—it's uncomfortable!"
We started with just 60 seconds a day, noticing the feeling of his feet on the floor or the temperature of his hands.
Over several weeks, Marcus noticed that his urge to zone out during conflict or stress was actually his body going into "freeze."
One day, after a fight with his partner, instead of storming out or shutting down, Marcus took a few slow breaths, named three colors he could see, and squeezed a pillow.
"It felt weird at first," he admitted. "But I didn't check out—I stayed present. And the world didn't end. My body calmed down. I realized I could actually ride the wave, and it passed." These small mindful pauses became his anchor—and slowly, the urge to escape softened, making space for real connection.

## Mindfulness Practices to Try

### 1. The 5-4-3-2-1 Grounding Exercise:

Notice…

- 5 things you can see
- 4 things you can touch
- 3 things you can hear
- 2 things you can smell
- 1 thing you can taste

This anchors you in the present and soothes an activated nervous system.

### 2. Breath Awareness:

Gently bring your attention to your breath.
Notice the inhale, the exhale.
Don't change anything at first—just observe.
If it feels supportive, try a gentle breath in for 4, out for 6, to signal safety to your body.

### 3. Mindful Self-Talk:

When you notice a trigger or anxious thought, pause and say to yourself:
"This is just a moment. I am safe right now."

## Somatic Practices to Try

**Body Scan:**

Starting at the crown of your head, slowly scan down your body, noticing any areas of tension, warmth, tingling, or ease.
Thank your body for any messages it gives you.
Search for body scans on YouTube to be guided through the process.

**Safe Touch:**

Place your hand over your heart or belly and take a few slow breaths.
Notice any feelings of warmth or comfort, even if small.
If it feels right, add a gentle affirmation:
"I am here for myself."

**Gentle Movement:**

Stand up and gently shake out your hands, arms, and legs for 30 seconds.
This can release tension, reset your energy, and bring you back into your body.

**Orienting:**

Look around the room and find something that feels comforting or beautiful.
Let your eyes rest there for a few breaths, letting your system know you are safe.

### Additional Practice: Micro-Mindfulness Check-Ins

Set a timer on your phone 2–3 times a day.
When it goes off, pause for just 60 seconds.

- Feel your feet on the ground.

- Take one full breath.

- Ask, "What's real for me right now?"

- Name one thing you're grateful for, or something you sense (sound, color, texture).

These tiny moments add up and help build a habit of being in the here and now, rather than in old stories.

### Advanced Exercise: "Mindful Movement Ritual"

Try adding gentle, intentional movement (QiGong, yoga, stretching, slow dance, even walking) to your mindfulness routine:

- As you move, focus on the sensation of muscles, joints, and breath.

- With each movement, silently repeat:

    "I am safe in my body. I am present here and now."

- Notice if any emotion or memory comes up. Thank your body for sharing, and move gently through it.

**My First Steps Toward Being Present**

Mindfulness used to feel like a kind of "dumb" practice to me, I really didn't see the point of it until I took a Certified Mindfulness Teaching course early into my hypnotherapy training. The first time I truly tried grounding—just noticing the colors in my room, the feel of my breath, the touch of my own hand—I realized that presence was possible, one small moment at a time.

I learned the point of practicing mindfulness and playing with these various "dumb" practices and it all clicked! I finally understood that in order to heal, I needed to start noticing, with curiosity and compassion vs judgment, to notice my thoughts, feelings (both mental and physical), and learned to connect with myself and my body. I found mindful movement like QiGong was among my favorite practices.

It didn't fix everything overnight, but it gave me a way to anchor myself. With every gentle practice, I learned that I could feel safe here and now, even if only for a few seconds at first.
That was the beginning of everything shifting.

**Journaling/Reflection Prompts**

- What does it feel like in my body right now?

- When was the last time I felt truly present and safe, even briefly?

- Which mindfulness or somatic practice feels most approachable to me today?

- What shifts for me when I pause, breathe, and notice this moment?

- What happens in my body and mind when I let myself slow down and "just be" for a moment, without needing to fix or judge anything?

**Affirmation for This Chapter:**

**"Presence is my power. I am safe to be here, now."**

## Gentle Reminder

You don't have to do these practices perfectly, or all at once. Even one mindful breath, one moment of grounding, or a simple pause is enough to begin building a new sense of safety and presence.
With every practice, you're teaching your body and mind that it's possible to be safe in the present.

## Coming Next: Chapter 6 —

How to nurture and reparent your inner child, meeting needs that were once unmet and building a new foundation of safety and love from the inside out.

# CHAPTER 6:

# REPARENTING YOUR INNER CHILD— BUILDING THE SAFETY YOU NEVER HAD

### Why Inner Child Work Matters

Inside each of us lives a younger self: The child who longed for safety, love, understanding, and acceptance. The child who maybe felt invisible, too much, not enough, or never quite "right."

When you have Disorganized (Fearful-Avoidant) or Dismissive (Avoidant) patterns, that inner child often still runs the show—especially when you're triggered, scared, or lonely.

**Reparenting** is the art of becoming the loving, consistent presence you always needed. It's how you break the cycle of unmet needs and begin building a foundation of secure self-connection.

### The Science of Inner Child Healing and Reparenting

Why does inner child work have such a powerful effect?

- **Attachment science** shows our earliest relationships literally wire our brain for either connection or self-protection. When those relationships are marked by inconsistency, neglect, or fear, our "emotional brain" (the limbic system, especially the amygdala and hippocampus) stores memories of what's dangerous and what's safe.

- When you revisit and nurture your inner child with present-day compassion, you activate the **prefrontal cortex** (the part of your brain that offers adult perspective, empathy, and self-regulation).

- Visualization and loving self-talk can actually lay down new neural pathways—overriding old "scripts" of shame or self-blame, and giving your nervous system a felt sense of safety.

- Regular "reparenting" can reduce stress hormones, increase resilience, and improve overall well-being—because you're practicing secure attachment, even if you never received it as a child.

## What Does Reparenting Mean?

Reparenting isn't about blaming your caregivers—it's about recognizing what was missing, and choosing to offer it to yourself now.

It means:
- Listening to your feelings with kindness, not criticism

- Meeting your needs for comfort, encouragement, and support

- Setting gentle boundaries for your own safety and well-being

- Speaking to yourself with patience and love

- Allowing your playful, creative, and sensitive sides to exist without shame

## The Unmet Needs of the Avoidant Inner Child

For Disorganized (Fearful-Avoidant) and Dismissive (Avoidant) people, the inner child often learned:

- "My feelings aren't important."

- "It's not safe to need or depend on anyone."

- "I have to handle everything alone."

- "I shouldn't bother people with my emotions."

- "I'll be punished or rejected if I show my true self."

These beliefs may have protected you, but now they keep you distant from yourself and others.
Reparenting is the antidote.

## Client Story: Anna's Turning Point

"Anna" (not her real name) always prided herself on being independent and capable. But inside, she often felt like a scared little girl—anxious to please, but quick to shut down or lash out if she felt misunderstood.
When Anna started reparenting work, she resisted the idea of "talking to herself like a child." It felt silly and awkward. But after a particularly tough week, she tried writing a letter to her seven-year-old self, who'd once been told, "You're too sensitive. Toughen up." As she wrote, Anna realized how lonely and unseen she'd felt as a child. She wrote words of comfort and encouragement she'd never received: "You're not too sensitive. You're beautifully aware. You matter just as you are."
The first few times, Anna cried—then felt strangely lighter. Over months, Anna practiced imagining giving her younger self a hug, or saying, "I'm here. I see you." She noticed she became less critical, more forgiving, and more able to accept love from others—one gentle step at a time.

## The First Time I Chose to Show Up for Myself

I used to think being strong meant never needing anyone, not even myself. But as I began reparenting work, I realized I'd left parts of myself—my scared, sad, playful, and creative parts—out in the cold.

One day, after a difficult conversation, I felt my old urge to shut down and push away my feelings. But instead, I sat with my journal and wrote a letter to my younger self. I told her she was allowed to feel whatever she felt, that she didn't have to hide, and that I was here to listen.

In that moment, I felt a wave of relief and softness inside me. I realized I could be the loving parent I'd always wanted. The more I practiced, the safer I felt in my own skin—and the easier it became to let others in.

## Reparenting Practices

### 1. Inner Child Letter Writing:

Write a letter to your younger self.
Tell them what you wish they'd heard growing up:
"You are enough. Your feelings make sense. I'm here for you, always."

### 2. Inner Child Visualization:

Close your eyes and imagine your younger self sitting beside you.
See yourself offering them a warm hug, gentle words, or simply your presence.
Let them know they are safe with you.

### 3. Daily Check-Ins:

Ask yourself each morning:
- How do I feel today?

- What do I need right now?

- How can I show myself care or comfort in this moment?

### 4. Play and Creativity:

Give your inner child space to play—draw, dance, sing, color, or just be silly for a few minutes.
Notice how this lightens your mood and helps you reconnect.

### Practices and Exercises

### 5. "Gentle Boundary Setting" (Somatic Reparenting):

- Place your hands out in front of you, palms facing forward, and say aloud:
  "I am allowed to have boundaries. I protect myself with love."

- Imagine a gentle light surrounding you, a safe space you can return to anytime.

### 6. "Reparenting Ritual" for Bedtime:

- Before sleep, sit with one hand on your heart, one on your belly.

- Whisper to yourself:
  "You are safe now. I am here, and I will take care of you."

- Imagine tucking your inner child in, offering comfort and reassurance.

### 7. "Soothing Self-Talk on the Go":

- The next time you notice your inner child's beliefs ("I'm too much," "I have to do it alone"), silently or quietly say:
  "It's safe to need support. I am here for you now."
  Pair this with a calming breath or gentle touch.

## Healing for Both Avoidant Styles

- **Disorganized (Fearful-Avoidant):** Focus on gentle consistency, reassurance, and validating your feelings—even when they're messy or contradictory.

- **Dismissive (Avoidant):** Focus on honoring your needs and emotions, and practicing receiving care (even if it feels awkward or "unnecessary" at first).

## Journaling/Reflection Prompts

- If I could speak to my younger self right now, what would I say?

- What did I need as a child that I didn't receive enough of?

- How can I give myself a bit of that today?

- What playful or creative activities make me feel most alive?

- When does my "inner child" feel most present in my life?

- How does my body respond when I offer comfort or permission to feel?

## Affirmation for This Chapter:

**I am the loving parent I always needed.
I am safe, I am loved, and I belong.**

## Bonus Practice: Inner Child Meditation— Meeting Your Younger Self

Find a comfortable position. You can sit or lie down, whatever feels safe and easy for you. If it's comfortable, close your eyes and bring your attention to your breath. Take three slow, gentle breaths—in through your nose, out through your mouth.

As you settle in, imagine a soft, warm light around your heart. With each breath, let this light grow a little brighter and bigger, filling your chest with warmth, gentleness, and acceptance.

Now, in your mind's eye, picture yourself as a child. There's no right or wrong image—maybe you see yourself at a particular age, or just sense your younger self nearby.

Notice how your inner child appears today. What are they feeling? What are they wearing? Where are they—inside or outside, at home or somewhere else?

Take a moment to greet your inner child. You might say, "Hello, I see you. I'm here with you now."

Imagine kneeling down to their level, letting them know you're here to listen and care for them. Maybe you offer a gentle smile, a warm hug, or simply your presence.

If they have something to say, listen with patience and an open heart. If they don't want to speak, that's okay too—just be with them.

Now, gently let your inner child know:
"You are safe with me. You are allowed to feel whatever you feel. I love you, and I will always be here for you."

If it feels right, imagine holding their hand or embracing them, letting your love and reassurance flow through that connection.

When you feel ready, imagine your inner child's light blending with yours, integrating that softness and warmth into your heart. Know that you can return to this safe place anytime you need.

Take a few more slow breaths, gently return your awareness to the present moment, and open your eyes when you're ready.

Pause for a moment and notice: How do you feel? What shifted inside you?

## A Gentle Note on Overwhelm

Sometimes, connecting with your inner child can bring up strong emotions, memories, or even discomfort. This is completely normal. Healing is a process, and you do not have to go through it alone. If you find yourself feeling overwhelmed, sad, anxious, or disconnected during or after this meditation, please honor what you need. It's okay to pause, to take a break, or to come back another time.
You may find it helpful to talk to a trusted friend, therapist, coach, or support group about your experience. Reaching out for support is a strength, not a weakness. You deserve kindness and care as you heal.
If you ever feel you'd like guidance or compassionate support as you walk this path, I am here for you. You're welcome to connect with me—whether for a session, a question, or just to share your experience. You can find me at ZenMindMichelle.com.

## Coming Next: Chapter 7 —

How to build safe, supportive relationships with others—one small, courageous step at a time.

# Chapter 7:

# Building Safe Relationships—
# What to Look For, What to Practice

**Why Safe Relationships Matter**

Healing from avoidant attachment doesn't happen in a vacuum. We heal in connection—with ourselves first, and then with safe, supportive others. For people with Disorganized (Fearful-Avoidant) or Dismissive (Avoidant) attachment, even the idea of trusting someone can feel risky or unfamiliar. But true healing involves learning how to recognize safety, both in others and in yourself, and practicing small acts of connection.

**The Science of Safe Connection**

From a neuroscience perspective, our brains and nervous systems are wired to need connection. The vagus nerve, oxytocin (the "bonding hormone"), and the brain's social engagement system all play key roles in helping us feel safe with others.
When we are around safe, consistent, and emotionally available people, our nervous systems learn to downshift from hypervigilance into calm and trust. With repetition, these experiences help rewire the brain for security.

**What Are "Green Flags" in Relationships?**

If you grew up with inconsistency or learned to mistrust closeness, you might be more familiar with *red flags*—signs of what to avoid—than with green flags, the subtle signals of safety.
 Learning to recognize green flags is essential for building secure, healthy relationships.

**Examples of Green Flags:**

- You feel calm, relaxed, or at ease around the person (even if just a little).

- They respect your boundaries, and don't pressure you to move faster than you're ready for.

- You can say "no" or express a need, and it's met with understanding (not punishment or guilt).

- The person apologizes and takes responsibility when they make a mistake.

- They show up when they say they will, and follow through on promises.

- You feel seen, heard, and valued—even if you disagree sometimes.

- You can share feelings or vulnerabilities and feel safe to do so.

- They celebrate your growth and support your healing, rather than feeling threatened by it.

- You don't feel like you have to hide parts of yourself to keep the relationship.

**Practice:**

Take a moment to reflect:

- Which green flags have I experienced in my relationships, even if only once or twice?

- Which ones am I still learning to recognize or trust?

## Building Relationship Safety—Mantras and Mindsets

When your system is used to danger or withdrawal, safety can actually feel "boring" or even uncomfortable at first. That's normal! You're not doing it wrong—your body and mind are simply adjusting to a new, healthier reality.

### Relationship Safety Mantra:

*"It is safe for me to connect with safe people. I am allowed to take things slow. I can trust myself to notice what feels good, and to step back if something feels wrong."*

Repeat this to yourself as needed, especially when navigating new or uncertain relationships.

### Practices for Cultivating Safe, Secure Relationships

1. **Micro-Risks:**
   Practice sharing one small truth, need, or feeling with someone you trust—even if it's just, "I'm feeling a bit anxious today." Notice how it feels in your body before, during, and after.

2. **Co-Regulation:**
   When you're with someone safe, see if you can sync your breath or heartbeat (e.g., sitting quietly together, holding hands, or even just sharing a smile). This helps both nervous systems feel more calm and connected.

3. **Boundary Practice:**
   Choose a small boundary to practice setting (e.g., "I need a little time alone tonight," or "I'm not ready to talk about that yet"). Celebrate any moment where your boundary is respected—this is evidence of safety!

4. **Reflect on Past Relationships:**
   Without judgment, review your past connections. Can you spot any green flags, moments of repair, or times you felt safe? What helped you recognize them?

5. **Repair After Rupture:**
   Every relationship has ruptures—misunderstandings, conflicts, or moments of distance. What matters most is the repair. Practice apologizing, asking for what you need, or simply saying, "Can we try that conversation again?"

**Client Story:**
**Choosing Safe Connection**

"Emily" (not her real name) had always chosen partners who were emotionally unavailable or critical. She didn't even realize safety was possible in a relationship. In our work, we practiced noticing small moments of calm with friends and even as she worked with me.

After months of gentle risk-taking, Emily started dating someone who was consistent and kind. At first, she felt bored and anxious—no drama! She was tempted to sabotage it, but remembered our mantra: "Safety is allowed to feel unfamiliar."

One night, after a difficult conversation, her new partner said, "Thank you for telling me what you need. I want to get this right with you." Emily burst into tears—she had never experienced repair or acceptance after a disagreement.

With time, Emily learned that safety wasn't just possible; it was what her heart had been longing for all along.

## Journaling/Reflection Prompts

- What are my personal green flags? How do I know when I feel safe with someone?

- What makes it hard for me to trust safety? What stories or memories come up?

- What would it feel like to allow myself to take small, safe risks in relationships?

- Who in my life today feels like a green flag person, even if it's just in small ways?

### Affirmation for This Chapter:

*"I am worthy of safe, loving connection.
I am learning to recognize and receive healthy love,
one moment at a time."*

## Coming Next: Chapter 8 —
When triggers happen—growing through setbacks and emotional storms, and how to keep returning to your center, no matter what life brings.

# CHAPTER 8:

# WHEN TRIGGERS HAPPEN—
# GROWING THROUGH SETBACKS
# AND EMOTIONAL STORMS

**Healing Isn't Perfect—And That's Okay**

No matter how much work you do on yourself, triggers will happen. You'll get reactive, shut down, pull away, or fall into old thought loops. You might even feel like you're "back at square one." This is not failure. It's life—and it's learning.

For those with Disorganized (Fearful-Avoidant) and Dismissive (Avoidant) patterns, it's especially easy to slip into self-blame, shame, or hopelessness after a trigger. But these moments are not signs you're broken—they're invitations to practice new tools, offer yourself grace, and keep going.

**What is a Trigger?**

A trigger is any experience—big or small—that sets off an old pattern of fear, avoidance, shutdown, or anxiety. It might be a tone of voice, a look, a word, or even a text message that reminds your nervous system of past pain. When you're triggered, your body often reacts before your mind even knows what's happening.

You may notice:

- Sudden tension, anxiety, or numbness

- Urges to withdraw, lash out, or "fix" everything immediately

- Old thoughts like, "Here we go again," "I can't trust anyone," or "I'll never get this right"

## The Neuroscience of Triggers and Setbacks

When you're triggered, your brain's **amygdala** fires up—this is your threat detection center, responsible for scanning for danger and keeping you safe. It can't tell the difference between a real threat today and an echo of past pain. That's why your body reacts before you can think it through—fight, flight, freeze, or fawn.

Your **prefrontal cortex** (the "wise adult" brain) goes partially offline when you're highly triggered. That's why it can be so hard to "logic" your way out of an emotional storm.

The good news?

Every time you soothe your nervous system and offer yourself compassion, you literally help your prefrontal cortex re-engage, and you lay down new neural pathways for recovery and resilience.

**With repetition, your brain learns: "I can have a trigger and still return to safety."**

## Normalizing Setbacks

Setbacks are normal. Healing isn't a straight line—it's more like a spiral, with progress and revisiting old wounds along the way. Every time you respond with a little more self-compassion, every time you notice the pattern sooner, you're growing—even if you don't feel like it in the moment.

## Client Story:
## Breaking the Spiral

"Jenna" had spent years avoiding conflict. Anytime her partner raised their voice or got frustrated, Jenna would immediately shut down—sometimes running to the bathroom to hide, sometimes going cold and distant for days.

In our work, Jenna learned to notice the first signs of a trigger: a pit in her stomach, clenched fists, a wave of "get out now!" She started practicing what we called the "Name and Pause"—saying to herself, "This is a trigger, not a threat. I'm safe right now."

At first, Jenna still went numb, but instead of disappearing completely, she would text a supportive friend or take a few slow breaths in another room. Over time, she began to recover faster, reconnect with her partner, and even share what she was experiencing. "I thought setbacks meant I was failing," Jenna said. "But now I see that every time I come back to myself—even just a little—I'm building new trust inside. My triggers are less scary now."

**Finding My Way Through a Trigger**

I used to think setbacks meant I had failed. One day, after an argument with someone close to me, I shut down completely. My mind went blank, my body felt frozen, and all I wanted to do was run away. In the past, I would have criticized myself or pretended nothing was wrong. But this time, I took a few slow breaths and gently named what was happening: "I'm triggered right now. I feel scared and small."

Instead of running, I reached out to a friend and shared how I was feeling. I let myself rest and didn't force myself to "fix it" right away. By the next day, I felt a little softer, a little safer, and a lot more human. Every time I move through a trigger with kindness—rather than self-blame—I build a little more trust in myself.

**Tools for Navigating Triggers and Setbacks**

**1. Name It, Don't Shame It**

When you notice a trigger, try saying (out loud or in your mind): "This is a trigger. I am safe to feel it."

## 2. Pause and Breathe

Step away from the situation if you can.
Take five slow, grounding breaths. Feel your feet on the floor.

## 3. Soothe Your Body

Use any calming technique from earlier chapters—touch, grounding, breath, safe movement.

## 4. Offer Yourself Kind Words

"It's okay to struggle. I am learning."
"This is an old wound, not a current danger."
"I am allowed to begin again, as many times as I need."

## 5. Repair and Reconnect

When you're ready, return to the person or situation if needed. Apologize if necessary, or share what you felt and needed.

## 6. Reflect

After the storm passes, journal or talk with someone you trust.
Ask: What set me off? What did I need in that moment? What can I do next time?

## What Makes Triggers "So Sticky"?

- **Emotional memory** is stored not only in your mind but in your body—especially if past pain or fear wasn't processed with support.

- When you're triggered, stress hormones like **cortisol** and **adrenaline** surge, making your reactions feel bigger and your thinking less clear.

- Each time you successfully return to calm, your nervous system learns that "it's possible to come back"—building resilience for next time.

- Over time, the window between "triggered" and "recovered" can shrink as your brain's wiring for self-soothing gets stronger.

**Additional Practices for Trigger Recovery**

**7. "The 90-Second Rule" (Dr. Jill Bolte Taylor's Neuro Tool)**
Intense emotional waves usually rise and fall within 90 seconds if you don't feed them with more thoughts or stories.

- When you notice a surge, start a timer or count slowly to 90.

- Breathe, ground, and simply feel what's happening in your body.

- Repeat: "I can ride this wave. It will pass."

**8. "Trigger Recovery Tap" (Somatic Exercise)**

- With your fingertips, gently tap your chest or collarbones while breathing slowly.

- As you tap, repeat a soothing phrase ("I am safe now," "This feeling will pass.")

- This activates both your body and mind, helping your system calm down and shift focus.

## 9. "Safe Place Visualization"

- Close your eyes and picture a place (real or imagined) where you feel completely safe and supported.

- Let your body and mind rest there, even for just a minute.

- Notice what shifts—what happens to your breath, your muscles, your thoughts?

## Gentle Reminders for Triggers

- Triggers are your nervous system asking for safety—not proof that you're unlovable.

- Progress is noticing triggers sooner, recovering faster, or simply being gentler with yourself each time.

- You are not alone—everyone gets triggered sometimes.

## Journaling/Reflection Prompts

- What does being "triggered" feel like in my body and mind?

- How have I handled triggers in the past? What helped (even a little)?

- What kind words or actions can I offer myself next time I feel overwhelmed?

- Who can I reach out to for support when I need it?

- How do I know when I'm coming out the other side of a trigger?

**Trigger Recovery Mantra**

"This is just a moment. I am safe, and I can choose compassion."

"My triggers are not failures—they are invitations to heal."

"I am not my past. I can pause, breathe, and begin again."

"Every trigger is a chance to bring love where I once felt fear."

Take a breath and repeat one of these to yourself whenever you feel overwhelmed, anxious, or pulled into old patterns. Let it be a gentle reminder: you are allowed to start again, as many times as you need.

**Affirmation for This Chapter:**

**"I am gentle with myself when old patterns appear. I am learning and growing every day."**

**Gentle Encouragement**

Remember, it's not about never getting triggered, but about recovering with more ease and self-kindness each time. Every single step, no matter how small, is forward movement.

**Coming Next: Chapter 9 —**
How to recognize and celebrate your progress, integrate your healing, and keep moving toward secure connection.

# CHAPTER 9:

# BECOMING SECURE— RECOGNIZING PROGRESS AND ANCHORING HEALING

**Progress Is Not Perfection**

You may not always notice your healing as it's happening.
Some days it feels like you're moving backwards.
But every small moment of awareness, self-compassion, or trying again is progress.

Healing Disorganized (Fearful-Avoidant) or Dismissive (Avoidant) patterns doesn't mean you never get triggered or avoidant again. It means you recover faster, judge yourself less, and choose connection—with yourself and others—more often than before.

**The Neuroscience of Progress: Why Noticing Wins Matters**

Your brain and nervous system are "wired for what's repeated"—whether that's old habits or new healing.

- Every time you notice and celebrate a small win, you activate the **reward system** in your brain (dopamine and oxytocin), creating a felt sense of success and safety.

- This rewires your neural pathways, making positive behaviors and secure attachment feel more natural over time.

- Neuroscience shows that *tracking progress* and *reflecting on growth* actually builds the brain's capacity for resilience and optimism—even for those with deep-rooted avoidance or trauma.

It's easy to focus on what's left to heal, but your system **needs to see and feel success**.

Celebrating progress isn't just "feel-good"—it's how your body and mind learn what's possible.

**The Power of Noticing Small Wins**

Examples of small wins:

- Noticing a trigger and pausing before reacting

- Sharing a feeling or need, even if your voice shakes (or you cry, like I do sometimes)

- Comforting your inner child after a tough day

- Setting a healthy boundary (even if it feels awkward)

- Allowing someone to support you, or accepting a compliment

- Catching yourself in an old thought and gently choosing a new one

Each of these moments is a step toward secure attachment.

**Celebrating the Little Victories**

In the past, I'd overlook or downplay my progress. If I wasn't "fully healed," it didn't count. But I started a habit of writing down every small win—even if it seemed insignificant. One day, I realized I hadn't shut down during an argument. Another day, I reached out for comfort instead of isolating.

Seeing those wins in writing reminded me: healing is happening, even when it's subtle. Over time, these small shifts became my new normal. I learned to trust myself and others more than I ever thought possible.

## The Science of Integration: Making Healing Stick

"Integration" means allowing your insights and healing to become part of your everyday life—body, mind, and spirit.

- **Repetition strengthens new neural pathways:**
  Every time you practice a new skill or habit (pausing, self-soothing, asking for support), your brain's "plasticity" grows. Over time, the new path becomes the default.

- **Emotion + attention = anchoring:**
  When you *feel* the success, pause, and savor it (even for 20 seconds), your brain "flags" the experience as important and more likely to be remembered and repeated.

- The more you practice celebrating wins and nurturing self-compassion, the more "secure" your nervous system becomes—even under stress.

### Integration Practices

**1. Win Journal**

Every day or week, jot down even the smallest healing actions or shifts. Over time, this becomes evidence of your growth.

**2. Anchoring Ritual**

After a positive experience (big or small), pause and let it sink in. Take three deep breaths, notice how your body feels, and say, "This is what healing feels like."

**3. Celebrate Yourself**

Choose a small way to honor your progress—light a candle, take yourself on a walk, share your win with someone you trust.

## 4. Reflect on Your Story

Look back at where you started and notice what's changed. What have you learned about yourself? What are you proud of?

## 5. Somatic Celebration Exercise

When you notice a win, take 20 seconds to *feel it in your body*: Smile, stretch, or put your hand over your heart and say, "This is what growth feels like. I am safe, and I am proud."

## Journaling/Reflection Prompts

- What's one way I've grown since starting this journey?

- What new patterns or choices have become easier for me?

- How can I celebrate myself today?

- What gives me hope for the future?

- How does my body feel when I pause to notice a win?

## Your Healing Roadmap: From Avoidance to Secure Connection

### 1. Awareness

Noticing your patterns, triggers, and automatic responses. Recognizing old stories and defenses with compassion. Realizing you are not broken—just beautifully adapted.

### 2. Understanding

Learning about Disorganized (Fearful-Avoidant) and Dismissive (Avoidant) styles. Understanding how the subconscious and nervous system shape your experience. Seeing the origins of your beliefs and behaviors.

## 3. Somatic & Mindful Presence

Practicing mindfulness to ground in the present.
Listening to your body and nervous system for cues of safety or threat. Using breath, grounding, and gentle movement to calm and center.

## 4. Reparenting the Inner Child

Offering compassion, validation, and care to younger parts of yourself. Meeting needs that were once unmet.
Building a foundation of self-trust and gentleness.

## 5. Practicing Connection with Others

Taking small, safe risks in relationships. Setting boundaries and expressing needs. Looking for "green flags" and celebrating secure, mutual connection

## 6. Navigating Triggers and Setbacks

Responding to old patterns with kindness, not shame.
Using tools to pause, soothe, and repair.
Remembering that progress is not perfection.

## 7. Celebrating Progress & Integrating Healing

Tracking small wins and growth. Creating rituals to anchor new experiences of safety and love. Allowing hope for a secure, connected future.

### You Are Here

No matter where you are on this roadmap, you are exactly where you need to be. Healing is a spiral—sometimes you'll revisit old steps, sometimes you'll leap ahead. Every step, every pause, every breath is part of your journey toward secure, loving connection.

**Pause. Celebrate. Breathe. You're doing beautifully.**

### Affirmation for This Chapter:

"Every small step is worth celebrating. I am proud of how far I've come."

**Coming Next: Final Chapter/Bonus Section —**

Daily practices for sustaining your healing and an invitation to keep growing with support and community.

# FINAL CHAPTER / BONUS SECTION:

# DAILY PRACTICES FOR LASTING HEALING & CONNECTION

**This Is Only the Beginning**

Finishing this book is not the end of your healing—it's the start of a new chapter. Everything you've learned is now a resource you can return to, again and again. Healing is an ongoing process, and every day brings a new opportunity to nurture yourself, deepen your connections, and create the secure life you desire.

**Daily Practices for Deepening Healing**

These simple rituals are designed to keep your nervous system, mind, and heart gently rewiring toward safety, connection, and joy.

**Remember: Small, repeated actions are what truly rewire your brain and body for secure attachment. You don't have to start doing all of these practices all at once! Pick one a day, get consistent with doing at least one, and then add more as you find the practices that you love doing!**

**1. Morning Check-In**

Upon waking, place a hand on your heart. Ask:

- How do I feel today?

- What does my body need right now?

- What gentle encouragement can I give myself this morning?

## 2. "Tiny Wins" Journal

Write down one small act of self-compassion, connection, or courage each day—even if it's just taking a breath before reacting. *Your brain needs to see and celebrate progress—this is neuroscience in action!*

## 3. 60-Second Grounding

Pause throughout your day to take three slow, mindful breaths. Notice your feet on the floor, your seat in the chair, or the sensation of your hand on your heart.

## 4. Affirmation or Mantra

Pick one phrase that feels good and repeat it:

- "I am safe now."

- "I am allowed to need, to love, and to be loved."

- "Each small step matters."

- "I am rewriting my story, one moment at a time."

## 5. Daily Boundary Practice

Say "yes" or "no" at least once today in alignment with your true needs, however small.
Notice how it feels in your body and mind.

## 6. Connect on Purpose

Reach out to one safe person—a friend, therapist, coach, or community—just to say hello or share something real. *Connection rewires the brain for safety—no step is too small.*

## 7. Evening Self-Tenderness

Before sleep, offer yourself gratitude:

- What did I do today that I'm proud of?
- How did I care for myself or try something new?
- What am I willing to forgive myself for today?

**New: The Science of Sustaining Change**

- Your nervous system learns through **repetition and safety**—every time you practice a grounding exercise or affirm your progress, you're wiring your brain for more resilience and calm.
- Reflecting on small wins and naming your feelings helps your prefrontal cortex stay engaged and strengthens your capacity for emotional regulation.
- Reaching out, even with a simple text or a smile, activates your social nervous system—making secure connection more familiar and less scary.

**Celebration Ritual: Anchoring Progress**

- After any moment of self-compassion, boundary-setting, or new connection, pause for 10–20 seconds.
- Feel the success in your body—breathe it in, let it settle.
- Say to yourself, "This is what healing feels like. I am becoming secure."

## A Closing Blessing

May you trust the pace of your healing,
May you see your courage in every step,
May you remember that love and safety are always available to you—
Within yourself, and in this world.
Go gently, and keep coming home to your heart.


**Remember: You're Never Alone**

Healing is courageous work. On the days it feels slow, or you slip into old patterns, return to your practices, your breath, and your self-compassion.

If you'd like more guidance to help you with daily mindfulness, somatic and journaling exercises, check out the companion guide "You Are Not Broken Companion: A Practical Integration Guide for Healing Avoidant Attachment"

Know that every moment of awareness and kindness counts.
If you ever need support, encouragement, or a safe space to continue this journey, I'm here for you.

Feel free to connect with me at ZenMindMichelle.com where you will find resources, a link to join my free community, information on coaching, or simply to share your story.

**Your healing matters. You matter.**

**Affirmation for the Journey:**

**"I am worthy of healing, connection, and love—
every single day."**

# THANK YOU

Thank you, from the bottom of my heart, for joining me on this healing journey.

Every page you've read, every exercise you've tried, and every moment you choose compassion over criticism is a powerful act of courage. Healing is not always easy, but it is always worthwhile. I honor the strength it takes to face your patterns and move toward greater connection, safety, and love.

If this book has spoken to you, know that you are not alone—there are many of us, walking this path of transformation, and it is a privilege to be connected with you here.

**The Clients I Love to Work With**

I am especially passionate about supporting people who:

- Feel stuck in cycles of avoidance, disconnection, or self-doubt—even after years of "trying to fix it" on their own.

- Are healing from childhood wounds, divorce, relationship struggles, or old patterns that just won't seem to budge.

- Are ready to deepen their self-awareness and reconnect with their inner wisdom and body.

- Want a safe, compassionate space to explore new ways of relating—to themselves, others, and life.

- Are open to blending practical, evidence-based tools with spiritual, intuitive guidance for true, holistic transformation.

If you're seeking support that honors all parts of you—mind, body, and soul—I would be honored to walk with you.

To stay connected, access free resources, or learn more about my programs, free Skool Community and other resources, visit www.ZenMindMichelle.com.

You're invited to download your free relaxation hypnosis recording and take your next step toward a life that feels secure, loving, and authentic.

With gratitude and encouragement,

Michelle Carbone

# ABOUT THE AUTHOR

**Michelle Carbone** is a Clinical Hypnotherapist, Intuitive Coach, and lifelong guide for those seeking healing, connection, and personal transformation. After nearly 25 years in a marriage marked by emotional disconnection, Michelle's own journey of awakening led her to uncover and heal deep-rooted patterns of avoidant and disorganized attachment.

Today, she blends subconscious reprogramming, mindfulness, somatic work, and compassionate coaching to help others move from emotional armor to authentic intimacy. Her approach is rooted in lived experience, trauma-informed methods, and the belief that no one is too far gone to find love — especially within themselves.

To work with Michelle or learn more, visit ZenMindMichelle.com

**Healing is a journey,
and you don't have to walk it alone.**

Made in the USA
Coppell, TX
09 January 2026

68751525R00056